D0681937

weblinks

You don't need a computer to use this book. But, for readers who do have access to the Internet, the book provides links to recommended websites which offer additional information and resources on the subject.

You will find weblinks boxes like this on some pages of the book.

weblinks

For more information about immigration, go to www.waylinks.co.uk /EthicalDebates/immigration

waylinks.co.uk

To help you find the recommended websites easily and quickly, weblinks are provided on our own website, **waylinks.co.uk.** These take you straight to the relevant websites and save you typing in the Internet address yourself.

Internet safety

↗ Never give out personal details, which include: your name, address, school, telephone number, email address, password and mobile number.

↗ Do not respond to messages which make you feel uncomfortable – tell an adult.

↗ Do not arrange to meet in person someone you have met on the Internet.

↗ Never send your picture or anything else to an online friend without a parent's or teacher's permission.

↗ If you see anything that worries you, tell an adult.

A note to adults
Internet use by children should be supervised. We recommend that you install filtering software which blocks unsuitable material.

Website content

The weblinks for this book are checked and updated regularly. However, because of the nature of the Internet, the content of a website may change at any time, or a website may close down without notice. While the publishers regret any inconvenience this may cause readers, they cannot be responsible for the content of any website other than their own.

WAYLAND

ETHICAL

DEBATES

Immigration

CATH SENKER

WAYLAND

First published in 2007 by Wayland

Reprinted 2008

Copyright © Wayland 2007

Wayland
338 Euston Road
London NW1 3BH

Wayland Australia
Level 17/207 Kent Street
Sydney, NSW 2000

Editor: Patience Coster
Series Editor: Camilla Lloyd
Consultant: Dr Jane Freedman
Designer: Rita Storey
Picture Researcher: Diana Morris

Acknowledgements:
p4 Kim Jones: *Socialist Worker*, 20 May
2006; p13 Yueksal Tuncay: BBC News, 30 Oct
2001 by Rob Broomby; p14 Arab News, Al-
Jazeerah, July 2003, www.aljazeerah.info; p22
Kobena: *Making the City Work: Low Paid
Employment in London*, 2005; p29
Pozzorubio: *Wall Street Journal*, 22 May
2001, © Dow Jones and Company Ltd; p33
(New York seamstresses) *Multinational
Monitor*, October 2001; p36 racist attack:
Cambridge Evening News, 16 December
2005, from www.islamophobia-watch.com;
p42 Peter Hitchens: 'The End of Britain?', in
Double Crossings: Migration Now (Index on
Censorship, 2003); p45 Priya Ruth Gully
Cole (author interview); p45 Faïza Guène:
Authortrek.com and *Socialist Review*,
May 2006.

Picture Acknowledgements: The author and
publisher would like to thank the following
for allowing their pictures to be reproduced
in this publication: Cover photograph:
Spectators (Chuck Savage/Corbis)
Rob Huibers/Panos Pictures: 1, 42, Sipa
Press/Rex Features: 4-5, 34, 35, 36, Khaled el
Fiqi/EPA/Corbis: 6, Keren Su/Corbis: 8, Mary
Evans Picture Library: 9, Bettmann/ Corbis:
10, Corbis: 11, Reuters/Corbis: 13, 15, David
H. Wells/Corbis: 16, Ed Kashi/ Corbis: 19, 24,
Peter Yates/Corbis: 20, Trygve Bolstad/Panos
Pictures: 21, 22, Caroline Penn/Corbis: 23,
Andrew Drysdale/Rex Features: 25, T &
L/Image Point/Corbis: 26, Howard Davies/
Exile Images: 27, Andy Johnstone/ Panos
Pictures: 28, Greg Smith/Corbis: 30, Steve
Raymer/ Corbis: 31, Jim Sugar/Corbis: 32,
Lorena Ros/Panos Pictures: 33, Justin
Jin/Panos Pictures: 37, Bob Krist/Corbis: 38,
John Nordell/Image Works/Topfoto: 39,
Nicholas Bailey/Rex Features: 40, Herbert
Pfarrhofer/ Corbis: 41, Paul Cooper/Rex
Features: 43, Ronnie Kaufman/Corbis: 44,
Tony Kyriacou/Rex Features: 45.

British Library Cataloguing in
Publication Data
Senker, Cath
    Immigration. - (Ethical debates)
    1. Emigration and immigration -
    Moral and ethical aspects -
    Juvenile literature
    2. Asylum, Right of -
    Juvenile literature
    I. Title
    172

ISBN-13: 978 0 7502 5027 6

Printed in China

Wayland is a division
of Hachette Children's Books,
an Hachette Livre UK Company.

contents

Real-life case study

This case study highlights some of the issues that surround the debate on immigration.

case study

Immigration and the law

On 1 May 2006, tens of thousands of people left school and work to attend mass protests around the USA. They were demonstrating against a new immigration law, known as HR 4437, that would make it harder for people to move to the USA and would increase security at the borders. One young woman on the protest of around half a million people in Los Angeles was Kim Jones: 'The day was amazing. I came all the way from Santa Ana [60 km/40 miles away] with my two friends on the metro. As soon as we got there all we saw was people wearing white in the streets. I could see everyone coming together as one, all fighting for one cause – blacks, Hispanics, whites, all sizes and all ages...'

'I'm not an immigrant – I was born in Los Angeles. But my parents struggled and put their lives on the line to come across the border. Those fences didn't stop them and now they're legal, but still I feel that what many people in the USA are thinking is totally unfair. Many US citizens say that immigrants need to get in line, that all they're doing is taking our money and our jobs. But immigrants have every right to be here, every right to want to live the "American dream".'

'We're all immigrants. If anything, the ones that deserve to be here are the Indians [the Native Americans]. But many people are ignorant and think that this place belongs to the whites, which is a total misunderstanding on their part.'

'I just felt as if I had to be there with my people. We are all humans, and no one is alien. No matter what, we should all be entitled to the same rights. Immigrants work and pay taxes on food and clothes. They are human just like all US citizens. If anything they should change the whole process of becoming legal because it takes 11 years and who really wants to wait that long?'

v i e w p o i n t s

'Many concerns that surround migration, such as loss of jobs, lower wages, increased welfare costs and the belief that migration is spiralling out of control, are not only exaggerated or unfounded but contrary to evidence.'
World Migration Report, 2005

'Large-scale immigration has brought enormous social upheaval to France, Germany, Britain and other European countries . . . an unblinkered society would seek to avoid such a fate. The only way to do so is to pursue a rigorous policy of immigration control.'
Immigration Control Platform, Ireland

It's a fact

Experts estimate that around 250,000-300,000 undocumented migrants (illegal immigrants, see pages 6-7) enter the USA each year, mostly from Mexico and Latin America.

▼ Crowds fill the streets at the demonstration of 1 May 2006 in New York City. Around the USA, immigrants and their supporters gathered for marches, prayers and demonstrations.

CHAPTER 1

What is immigration?

Migration – the movement of people from one country to another – occurs all the time and has done so throughout human history. Anyone who moves is a migrant. Immigration is a term used to describe the movement of people from their own country to settle permanently in another. They are immigrants to their new country, but have emigrated from their native country. In their home country, they are called emigrants. Legal immigrants are people who have permission to settle in their new country. Illegal immigrants (also called undocumented migrants) live in the new country illegally, according to immigration law. People who flee their country to escape war or persecution are known as refugees. If they have made a claim to stay in the country as refugees, they are also known as asylum seekers.

Push and pull factors

There are many reasons why people migrate. Some migration experts talk about 'push and pull' factors. Push factors are bad things that make people leave their country. Perhaps they have little chance of making a good living. Their country may be affected by natural disasters, such as earthquakes or floods, or by problems such as conflict, civil war or political persecution. The decision to migrate is difficult and painful. It means leaving behind family and friends and travelling

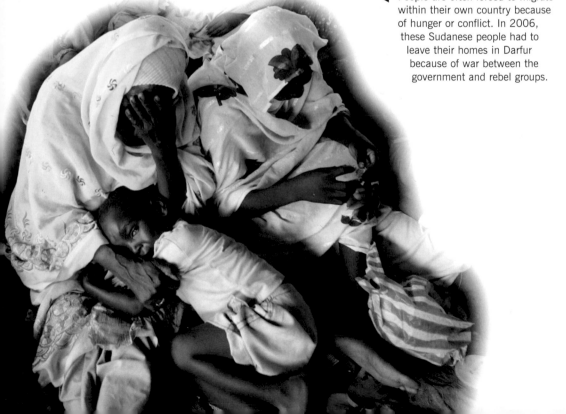

◀ People are often forced to migrate within their own country because of hunger or conflict. In 2006, these Sudanese people had to leave their homes in Darfur because of war between the government and rebel groups.

to an often-unknown destination. It is also expensive, so the decision is not taken lightly. Relatively few people leave their countries even if they are in a desperate situation – the poorest people are seldom the ones to move because they cannot afford to travel.

Pull factors are the things that attract people to the new country. People may hope for a better standard of living and improved healthcare and education services, or they may want to live in a country with more freedoms – to escape from persecution and danger. They may desire a better life for their children. One of the basic reasons for migration is that there is a huge wealth gap between More Developed Countries (MDCs) and Less Developed Countries (LDCs). For example, most immigrants to the USA and Canada come from poor countries and are seeking an improved standard of living. But there are just as many people moving between LDCs as there are moving to MDCs.

Forms of immigration

Some people move to another land as migrant workers. They go to earn money for a while and then return home. Immigrants move permanently to seek a better life. They may settle legally by applying to move to their chosen country and being accepted. Others are known as 'undocumented migrants' or 'illegal immigrants' because they have not entered the country according to the immigration laws. They may have arrived legally on a student or tourist visa (allowing the right to stay for a short time) and stayed on after their visa has run out. Or their situation might have become 'illegal' following changes in a country's immigration and residence laws.

People may be forced to escape their country as refugees because they fear for their lives owing to war, famine or persecution. Most refugees are from LDCs and live in other LDCs. Large numbers cross borders to a safer country and stay in refugee camps. The tiny minority able to reach MDCs must apply for asylum (the right to refuge). Sometimes the difference between refugees, migrants and immigrants is unclear. Some undocumented migrants are refugees who did not know how to claim asylum. Others are asylum seekers whose claim to refugee status has been rejected; these asylum seekers sometimes remain illegally rather than return to their home country.

weblinks

For more information about migration, go to www.waylinks.co.uk/Ethical Debates/immigration

summary

▶ There are many different reasons why people migrate to another country for a time, or immigrate as permanent settlers.

▶ More migrants actually move between LDCs than move from LDCs to MDCs.

▶ Some people believe that More Developed Countries are being 'swamped' by immigrants, who cause problems in society.

▶ These people believe it would be better to restrict immigration.

CHAPTER 2

The history of immigration

Since the earliest times, people have moved from place to place in search of better farmland or work possibilities. They have also migrated to escape natural disasters, such as floods, earthquakes or famine and to flee persecution. Throughout history, when new people arrived in a region they either settled peacefully or fought with the people already living there for control of the area. Sometimes rulers built walls to keep out invaders. In the third century BC, the Chinese emperor, Shih Huang-ti, built the Great Wall of China to stop the neighbouring tribes from attacking his lands. The Great Wall stretched 7,300 km (4,500 miles) from east to west. However, until the rise of the nation state (see below), there were no laws to govern who was allowed to live in which country.

Nations arise

From about 1500 onwards, European countries began to develop strong, central governments. A sense of national identity arose, along with the growth of national languages and religions. This sense of identity was accompanied by the idea that minority groups living in the countries were outsiders, and did not belong. For example, from the eighth century, much of Spain was under Muslim rule.

▼ Jinshanling Great Wall, 140 km (90 miles) north-east of Beijing, part of the Great Wall of China. The Great Wall was built in many stages over the centuries. A large part of the wall still exists today and is a major tourist attraction.

▲ Despite Queen Elizabeth I's attempt to expel the African population of England and Scotland, wealthy people, such as this group on a fishing trip in the 1780s, still kept African servants.

From the twelfth century onwards, Christian forces from the north of Spain gradually conquered the Muslim lands. In 1492, Spain was ruled by the Roman Catholic King Ferdinand and Queen Isabella. To reinforce the unity of their kingdom in accordance with their religion, they forced out Jewish and Muslim populations that had been living in Spain for centuries.

Another example of the expulsion of people seen as outsiders occurred in England. In the late sixteenth century, there were probably hundreds of Africans living in England and Scotland and working as servants and entertainers. In the 1590s, the harvests failed and poverty increased. The Protestant English queen, Elizabeth I, blamed the Africans for using up resources and declared that as non-Christians they were unwelcome. In 1596 and 1601, she issued orders that all Africans be expelled from England.

viewpoints

'. . . we order all Jews and Jewesses of whatever age they may be, who live, reside, and exist in our said kingdoms and lordships . . . that by the end of the month of July next of the present year, they depart from all of these our said realms and lordships . . .'
From the 1492 *Edict of Expulsion* from Spain, in which King Ferdinand and Queen Isabella accused the Jews of trying to convert Christians to Judaism

'. . . the Jews . . . are both in their origin and progress not otherwise to be regarded than under the common circumstance of human nature; if all professions were open to them they would betake themselves to Building, Farming and all sorts of Improvements like other people.'
Irish thinker, John Toland, writing in 1714; Toland believed that Jews should have the same rights as everyone else

▲ A group of freed slaves, photographed in a town in southern USA shortly after the civil war of the 1860s. In 1865, at the end of the war, slavery was abolished in the USA.

Colonialism and mass migration

Between 1500 and 1800, European powers expanded their trading networks across the world. In order to control the economies of the countries they traded with, they conquered them and became their rulers. This system became known as colonialism. European nations such as England, France, Spain and Portugal became colonial nations, and the lands they governed were their colonies.

The slave trade

From the sixteenth century, the Spanish, Dutch, English and French established vast plantations (farming estates) in the Americas to grow sugar, cotton and tobacco. They needed large numbers of workers for these plantations. As most of the native populations had either died fighting the colonial powers or from disease, the European powers enslaved people from their colonies in Africa to work for them. Between 1500 and 1870,

maybe 12 million Africans (the exact figure is not known) were shipped to the Americas from West Africa. The slaves were put to work under cruel conditions on the plantations or laboured, unpaid, as miners, soldiers and shipbuilders. This forced migration – the wrenching of people from their homes and families to be transported across the sea and exploited – became known as the Atlantic slave trade. It continued until the nineteenth century.

Another form of forced migration began in the eighteenth century. From 1788 until 1850, the British government sent convicts (people found guilty of crime) to Australia. Around 160,000 mostly English, but also Scottish and Irish men and women, were transported. Most of them had committed relatively minor offences but had been convicted several times. They were usually sentenced to between seven and 14 years, although some were sentenced to life in exile. These convicts built communities in Australia.

Between 1850 and 1950, there was a huge wave of voluntary international emigration. This was mostly made up of Europeans leaving for the USA, Canada, New Zealand and Argentina in search of a better life. Around 50 to 60 million people emigrated from Europe between 1800 and 1925.

Controls and quotas

From the late nineteenth century, richer nations with industrial economies, such as the USA, Canada and Britain, began to introduce laws to keep out immigrants they did not want. For example, in the USA, the Chinese Exclusion Act became law in 1882. In Britain, the 1905 Aliens Act fixed a limit on the number of Jews to be allowed in from eastern Europe. The US Immigration Act of 1924 allowed a quota of immigrants from each country, depending on the number of that group already in the USA. This quota was introduced in an effort to try to keep the proportion of various ethnic groups equal. Yet the quota did not apply to North America, so people could come freely from Mexico and Canada.

Then, in the 1930s, Europe and the USA were plunged into a deep economic crisis that became known as the Great Depression. High levels of unemployment resulted in countries introducing strict controls to limit immigration. Following the rise to power of the German Nazi leader, Adolf Hitler, in 1933 and during the Nazi occupation of much of Europe during the Second World War, Jews were persecuted and killed. Yet owing to immigration controls and anti-Semitism (hatred of Jews), few Jews were given refuge in either the USA or the European countries that remained free of Nazi rule.

▲ An elderly Russian Jewish immigrant at Ellis Island, New York, in 1900. Upon their arrival, all immigrants came to Ellis Island to be checked by officials.

World population growth by regions, 1850-1950

	1850 population in millions	1950 population in millions	Average annual growth (%)
Receiving (countries of mass immigration)			
Americas	59	325	1.72
North Asia	22	104	1.57
South-east Asia	42	177	1.45
Sending (countries of mass emigration)			
Europe	265	515	0.67
South Asia	230	445	0.66
China	420	520	0.21
Africa	81	205	0.93
World	1,200	2,500	0.74

Source: *Atlas of World Population History*

Immigration after the Second World War

During the Second World War (1939-45), more than 60 million people from Nazi-occupied Europe became refugees. Some of them were unable to return home afterwards. Following the war, the international community established a system to help refugees. The United Nations Refugee Convention of 1951 listed their rights to live, work and study freely in a safe country. Since then, there have been many wars that have led to large movements of people seeking refuge.

After 1945, in addition to the mass movement of refugees there was a huge movement of migrants who moved to seek a better life. In contrast with the situation in the 1930s, in the 1950s and 1960s European countries experienced a huge labour shortage and needed immigrants to help rebuild their shattered economies. Meanwhile, many former European colonies gained their independence. This was often a process that involved conflict, and the citizens of these colonies suffered from war and poverty. Western European governments encouraged immigrants to come from their former colonies and from southern Europe, the poorer region of the continent. Now mostly non-Europeans were on the move. In the 1950s, the UK, France and Belgium received 40,000 immigrant workers per year. In 1961, Germany invited 'guest workers' from Italy, Yugoslavia and Turkey to come and work for a few years. After the guest worker scheme ended in 1973, many workers stayed on in Germany.

From the 1960s onwards, the USA, Canada and Australia relaxed their immigration laws and allowed in more people from LDCs. For example, in 1967 Canada introduced a points system: potential immigrants were awarded points depending on their education, their fluency in English and French and on the need for their skills at the time. If they achieved the required number of points they could settle there regardless of where they were from.

At the same time in Europe, a decline in economic growth led governments to try to limit immigration. The UK passed restrictive laws in 1962, 1968 and 1971. However, existing immigrants to Europe were not forced to return to their countries of origin. There were further arrivals through family reunification programmes, which allowed spouses, parents and children to join their families. In the late twentieth and early twenty-first centuries, conflict, natural disasters and poverty in LDCs led to large numbers of people seeking a better life in MDCs.

It's a fact

In the UK in 1960-61, the Conservative government's minister for health, Enoch Powell, recruited Caribbean workers for the National Health Service (NHS). However, in the late 1960s, when the tide had turned against immigration and when the Conservatives were no longer in power, Powell inflamed prejudice against black people and called for a halt to immigration.

weblinks

For more information about migration to the UK, go to www.waylinks.co.uk/Ethical Debates/immigration

▲ A Turkish clothing shop in Berlin's Kreuzberg district, which is called 'Little Istanbul' because a large community of Turks live there. There are 2.4 million people of Turkish origin in Germany.

case study

Yueksal Tuncay

Yueksal Tuncay came to Germany from Turkey in the 1960s to work for the car manufacturer, Daimler Benz. He came as a guest worker, expecting to stay between ten and 15 years, but he did not go back to Turkey. Yueksal managed to save some money and set up a Turkish bakery in Berlin. Although happy running his own business in Germany, he still feels he is regarded as different: 'When I meet an official or a policeman, they see my black hair and to them I am still a foreigner'.

viewpoints

'I have set and always will set my face like flint against making any difference between one citizen of this country and another on grounds of his origin.'
Enoch Powell, 1964

'It almost passes belief that at this moment twenty or thirty additional immigrant children are arriving from overseas in Wolverhampton alone every week – and that means fifteen or twenty additional families of a decade or two hence . . . We must be mad . . . as a nation to be permitting the annual inflow of some 50,000 dependants.'
Enoch Powell, 1968

CHAPTER 3.

Is immigration out of control?

All MDCs have witnessed a huge increase in immigration since the Second World War, and some people believe that immigration has got out of hand. The increased use and low cost of air travel make it easy for people to move between countries. Many people argue that immigration was useful in the past, but now it should stop. For instance, since 1970, the foreign-born population of the USA has increased rapidly as a result of large-scale immigration, primarily from Latin America and Asia. As a percentage of the total population, the foreign-born population of the USA more than doubled from 4.7 per cent in 1970 to an estimated 9.7 per cent in 1997.

Views on immigration

	Good thing %	Bad thing %	Don't know %
From the Middle East and North Africa			
Great Britain	60	30	10
France	53	45	2
Germany	34	57	9
Spain	67	26	7
Netherlands	46	49	5
Poland	47	43	10
From Eastern Europe			
Great Britain	62	28	10
France	52	47	1
Germany	31	60	9
Spain	72	22	6
Netherlands	50	47	3
From former Soviet bloc			
Poland	44	46	10
From Asia			
USA	62	26	12
Canada	77	15	8
From Mexico and Latin America			
USA	60	29	11
Canada	78	15	7

Source: Pew Global Attitudes Project, 2005

case study

Fleeing persecution and poverty

Southern Spain is close to Morocco, at the tip of northern Africa. It is the destination of many northern and western African migrants desperate to flee conflict, persecution or poverty and to reach Europe.

Promise is a 26-year-old woman from Benin City in Nigeria. Her family paid for her to find a better life in Europe. Promise paid US$7,000 (£3,700) to people smugglers to get her to Morocco. Her journey took three months. She then had to wait five months in Morocco for the sea to become calm enough for her to make the journey to Europe. During this time she spent most of her savings. An increasing problem for many women in Promise's situation is that they are forced to work as prostitutes while they wait to travel the last leg of their journey to Europe.

Promise had heard that pregnant women were not deported (sent back to their country of origin) by the Spanish authorities. She was three months pregnant when she paid a further US$1,500 (£792) to make the crossing to Spain. She travelled with 35 others in a *patera*, a flimsy raft-like dinghy. Promise now lives in a small town in Andalucia, southern Spain, with her child and three other women from Benin City who were also pregnant when they arrived. But the majority of migrants who reach Spain are sent straight back.

▲ In 1999, these African migrants, five Nigerians and two from the Ivory Coast, hoped to reach Ceuta, a Spanish-ruled town in northern Morocco, in this small boat.

According to Eurostat, the statistical branch of the European Union (EU), the number of foreigners who had not become citizens of their new country and who were living in Western European EU nations was 22.9 million in 2004, or about 5.9 per cent of the population. That represents an increase of 56 per cent since 1990. And this figure does not include undocumented migrants.

There is also a massive movement of undocumented migrants from Mexico to the USA. Although experts estimate there are between 250,000 and 300,000 arrivals a year, others think the figure could be as high as one million. In addition, since immigrants tend to have larger families than members of the host population, the overall population increases even further. In 2006, the US fertility rate (the average number of children a woman has) was estimated at 2.09. Evidence published in 2005 by the Center for Immigration Studies indicates that Mexican women in the USA have an average of 3.5 children.

It's a fact

In 2005, a law known as HR 4437 was passed in the USA making all illegal immigration a crime. It did not offer a way for undocumented migrants already in the USA to become citizens. Plans for increased border security included the placing of cameras along the border with Mexico. Web users would be able to spot and report people trying to cross the border illegally.

Is immigration manageable?

Other people argue that immigration is less of a problem than many fear. They say that most people believe the level of immigration is higher than it actually is. There are about 192 million people living outside their country of birth, which is about 3 per cent of the world's population. Around half of all immigrants move to LDCs rather than MDCs.

In the USA, a major destination for immigrants, the total number of immigrants per year (including the estimated number of refugees and undocumented migrants) is lower than it was in the peak years of immigration to the USA in the early twentieth century.

▼ This Latin American worker is raking blueberries in Maine, USA. Farmers in the USA rely on migrant workers for labour.

Since then, the US population has more than doubled. And since those peak years the rate of immigration has fallen by around two-thirds. Although the foreign-born population of the USA has increased, in 2006 it was estimated that just 10 per cent of the total population was born outside the country. This does not indicate that the country is being 'swamped' by immigrants. While newspaper headlines highlight the number of immigrants flooding into a country, there are few headlines about the high level of emigration from MDCs.

People who believe that immigration is not a major problem point to the fact that large numbers of undocumented migrants go abroad for several years and then return home. They do not immigrate permanently. This is known as 'circular migration' and is typical of Mexican workers. Between 1965 and 1986, it has been estimated that around 28 million undocumented Mexicans entered the USA. Around 23 million of them, the great majority, eventually returned to Mexico. Immigration patterns also change over time. As countries develop, emigration slows down. Large numbers used to emigrate from countries such as South Korea and Ireland, but since these countries have developed their economies, they are now destinations for immigrants.

Big families?

Immigrant families tend to have larger families than members of the host population do. But the evidence shows that the fertility rate falls within a generation or so to match that of the host population. During 1991-98, migrant women in France had an average of 2.5 children compared with 1.7 among native-born French women. Women who had

arrived in France before they reached the age of 13 had only a slightly higher fertility rate, because they adopted the local preference for smaller families.

Net migration to the 15 countries of the EU in 2003, and to the USA in 2000. (Net migration is the difference between immigration into and emigration from a country.)

Country	Migration per 1,000 inhabitants
Austria	4.7
Belgium	3.4
Denmark	1.3
Finland	1.1
France	0.9
Germany	1.7
Greece	3.2
Ireland	7.8
Italy	10.4
Luxembourg	4.7
Netherlands	0.4
Portugal	6.1
Spain	17.6
Sweden	3.2
UK	4.4
USA	3.5

Source: *Europe in Figures*, 2005

weblinks

For more information about international migration, go to www.waylinks.co.uk/Ethical Debates/immigration

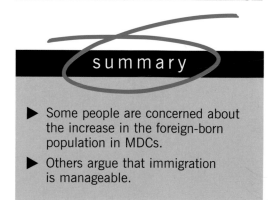

summary

▶ Some people are concerned about the increase in the foreign-born population in MDCs.

▶ Others argue that immigration is manageable.

CHAPTER 4

How immigration affects the host economy

Some people maintain that immigrants put pressure on scarce resources in the host country, such as housing, education and health services. The argument is that immigrants go to richer countries to take advantage of welfare systems that do not exist in their own countries. The new country then pays for the education of the immigrants' children and the care of their elderly relatives. This is unfair on local people.

Studies carried out in the USA in the early 1990s found that immigrants made slightly more use of welfare than local people did. This was because immigrants tended to be poorer. Although unemployment levels among immigrants are similar to the national average in the USA and Canada, in Europe levels are generally higher than those of the host population. A 2006 report from Sweden showed that there were higher rates of unemployment among people from immigrant families than among native Swedes, and that immigrants were more heavily dependent on social welfare benefits.

Environmental pressures

The anti-immigration lobby argues that there are environmental effects too. In the USA, the organization NumbersUSA campaigns to reduce the number of

It's a fact

According to a 2006 survey, illegal immigrants (undocumented migrants) in Italy are generally better educated than native Italians. The survey found that 41 per cent of those aged between 25 and 64 had a high-school diploma (showing that they had successfully completed secondary school) compared with 33 per cent of Italians in the same age group.

Immigration to European countries, 1999-2004

Year	Country	Percentage born in another country	Origin of largest group
1999	France	6%	Portugal
2003	UK	5%	Ireland
2003	Portugal	2%	Cape Verde
2004	Germany	9%	Turkey
2004	Spain	7%	Ecuador
2004	Italy	3%	Albania
2004	Netherlands	4%	Turkey
2004	Sweden	5%	Finland

Source: Eurostat, 2006

immigrants. It argues that immigration has caused a rise in population that has contributed to overcrowding in cities. Problems associated with overcrowding include urban sprawl (the unplanned growth of cities), traffic congestion, crammed schools and crowded outdoor recreation areas. In rural areas, the growing population contributes to loss of natural habitat and the destruction of prime farmland, as more houses and schools need to be built. In addition, greater numbers of people put pressure on limited energy and water supplies.

Some US environmentalists are particularly concerned because people in the USA consume resources at the highest rate of any country in the world. Therefore, the increase in the US population has a noticeable effect on the use of the world's resources.

The extremists' response

In several European countries, right-wing political groups have taken up people's concerns about population increase and expressed them in extreme terms. In 2006, the Italian government announced a plan to give legal status to 350,000 undocumented migrants who were working and had lived in the country for at least five years. Robert Calderoli, a senior member of the Northern League, a far-right political group, claimed that this would lead to 'an invasion' of migrants. Earlier he had said that Muslim immigrants were stealing jobs and homes from native Italians and that all undocumented migrants should be sent back to their country of origin. Some people say that, unless governments limit immigration, such views will become more popular and there will be growing conflict between local people and immigrants over access to resources, such as housing.

▼ A migrant worker and his family, near Watsonville, California, USA. Migrant workers are often paid low wages and forced to live in cramped conditions.

▲ Some people believe that unemployed workers, such as these people queuing up at an unemployment office in Pontiac, Michigan in the USA, have been put out of a job by immigrant workers.

Competing for jobs

Although the birth rate is declining in Europe, there is unemployment. Anti-immigration campaigners argue therefore that it is wrong to allow in large numbers of immigrants. Migration Watch UK is a pressure group that wants a reduction in immigration. Its chairman, Sir Andrew Green, noted in 2006 that although Britain had a strong economy, 4.2 million people were unemployed or receiving incapacity benefit because they could not work. Green said that letting in foreign labourers makes it difficult for the government to reach its goal of returning one million Britons to work. Immigrants compete for jobs with local people, who lose their jobs or remain unemployed.

Such campaigners argue that this problem becomes more severe when the economy is in a downturn and fewer workers are needed. Professor Vernon M. Briggs at Cornell University, USA, says that the number of undocumented migrants (estimated at 11.5 to 12 million in the USA in 2006) is the real problem. They take work from young people looking for their first job and from older ethnic minority workers with few skills.

A related argument is that immigrants are prepared to work for lower than average wages. This allows employers to reduce wages in general for all workers. One economist, George Borjas of Harvard University, USA, maintains that poorly educated men who had dropped out of high school saw their earnings decrease by 7.4 per cent between 1980 and 2000 as a result of competition from immigrants for jobs.

European Union expansion

In May 2004, the European Union expanded to include ten more countries, increasing the total number of its member states from 15 to 25. At first, only the UK, Ireland and Sweden allowed in immigrants from the new EU nations as part of an agreement to permit freedom of travel within the union. By August 2006, more than 427,000 immigrants had arrived in the UK from the new member states – rather more than the 13,000 a year that had been predicted by the government!

One of the immigrants, a 30-year-old hairdresser, Agnieszka Skretkowicz, came to London from Poland because she could not make a living at home. 'I love Poland; it's a beautiful country,' she says, 'but it's hard there.' In 2006, Finland, Spain and Portugal announced they would lift restrictions on eastern European immigrants. Migration Watch UK asserts that unless Germany, France, Austria and Italy also open their doors, the UK could be overwhelmed with immigrants, especially when Romania and Bulgaria join the EU in 2007.

It's a fact

Out of more than 427,000 eastern European workers in the UK in 2006, 82 per cent were aged between 18 and 34. Of these, 1,777 had applied for income support because they could not earn enough money to live on, while 3,519 had applied for unemployment benefits because they had lost their jobs.

weblinks

For more information about groups lobbying against immigration, go to www.waylinks.co.uk/Ethical Debates/immigration

▼ This Filipino man works on a Norwegian car ferry. In order to work in Norway for more than three months, people from outside the Nordic countries need to have a special work visa.

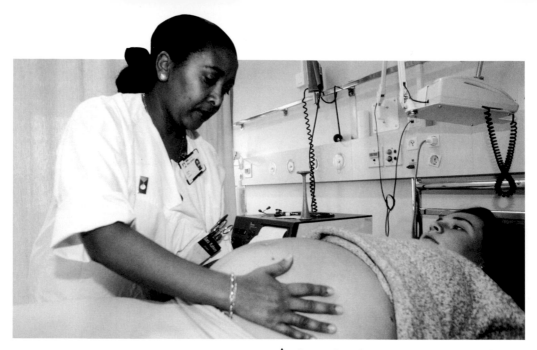

Contributing to the national wealth

People in favour of immigration argue that both skilled and unskilled immigrants give more than they take from the economy in the long term. The US National Academy of Sciences has found that each immigrant, with his or her descendants paying taxes, will contribute US$80,000 (£42,220) to the national budget. Undocumented migrants (who avoid contact with the authorities so they are not detected) receive no welfare benefits, yet still pay tax. In the USA, for example, some of them have fake social security numbers in order to get jobs, and so they pay tax on their earnings. They pay sales tax on clothes, petrol and other goods they buy. Therefore, immigrants help to pay for housing, education and welfare.

The pro-immigration lobby argues that, since governments benefit from the immigrants' contribution, they should use taxes sensibly to ease the stress on scarce resources. They should plan urban development and provide public transport to ease traffic problems. They should build enough houses and schools and protect farmland.

▲ Sara, a Somali migrant, works as a midwife in a hospital in Oslo, Norway. There are many vacancies for nurses in Norwegian hospitals. For locals nursing is a low-paid job, but for migrants from LDCs the salary seems high.

case study

A low-paid worker in London

A survey published in 2005 showed that most cleaners on London's Underground (metro) network were from African countries, especially Nigeria and Ghana. Kobena is a university graduate from Ghana. Since arriving in the UK in 2003, he has worked as a cleaner on the Underground for 54 hours a week. He earns the official minimum rate of £5.05 (US$9.5) per hour, considerably less than half of the average earnings in the city. The job allows only 12 days' paid holiday a year and no sick pay. Kobena even has to pay to travel on the Underground to carry out his job. He supports four children in the UK and also sends money to his family in Ghana. Kobena feels his employer shows no concern for workers' welfare: 'They just want us to work.'

Employment

Pro-immigration campaigners state that the number of jobs in the economy is not fixed, so it is untrue that immigrants take work away from locals. They say that immigrants often create new businesses and provide jobs. In most countries, foreign workers tend to take low-paid jobs in construction, agriculture and in the service industries – jobs that locals do not want. They may take these low-paid jobs even if they are highly qualified. They fill in the gaps in the workforce. For example, in the UK and Scandinavia they take up vacancies in the health and education sectors. Between 2002 and 2003, more than 40 per cent of new nurses registered in the UK came from overseas. Much of the UK's hotel industry relies on the labour of undocumented workers.

Even when unemployment is high, it is argued, immigrants do not make the problem worse. Local people who lose their jobs will probably draw unemployment benefit until they find suitable work. Immigrants in this situation are more likely to take on any casual work they can find, for example, as cleaners or building labourers.

▼ A Polish plumber working in a London house: between May 2004 and June 2006, Polish people made up more than half of migrants to the UK from EU states.

Surveys in MDCs such as Germany, Australia, Canada, the USA and the UK have concluded that an influx of immigrants makes little difference to employment or wage levels for the host population. In the USA, a 2006 study found that immigrant workers complement rather than compete with US-born workers. The foreign-born workers occupy the lowest paying, unskilled jobs while the US-born workers move on to more rewarding jobs.

viewpoints

'If you allow more unskilled workers into the US, it will lower costs for employers. It will also lower wages for people who do those jobs. It's clearly a political question. If you want to benefit low-skill American workers, you reduce illegal immigration.'
Professor Peter Cappelli, Wharton University of Pennsylvania

'The presence of illegals [illegal immigrants] is not associated with higher unemployment among natives . . . Geographically, it tends to be the reverse: places with large numbers of illegals tend to have lower unemployment than places without illegals. Illegals go where the economies are strong.'
Jeffrey S. Passel, Pew Hispanic Center

Boosting the working population

Europe's population is declining. In the EU the average fertility rate is 1.4 children per woman, but a country needs an average fertility rate of 2.1 children per woman to maintain its population at the same level. The European population is also ageing, which means there is an increasing number of old people compared with people of working age. Countries need large numbers of workers to pay taxes towards pensions for the elderly and to care for them. Immigrants, who are mostly young, can help address the labour shortage problem. So, the pro-lobby argues, it is right to allow in immigrants.

Spain has the lowest fertility rate in Europe (1.2 children per woman). In 2005 it had 3.7 million immigrants, representing 8.5 per cent of the population. The largest immigrant group is from Ecuador. Ecuadorians have been coming to Spain since a severe economic crisis hit their country in 1999. They speak Spanish and integrate easily into the workforce. Officially there are 476,000 Ecuadorians in Spain, but there are also many undocumented migrants. The women often work as housekeepers and nannies, while Ecuadorian men work in industry, construction, commerce and agriculture.

Reducing the labour shortage

The situation in Spain is typical of European countries. The French Institute of International Relations has predicted that Europe must admit 30 million immigrants by 2020 or face a drop in the production of goods, which would damage its economies. The MDCs are trying to recruit skilled migrants to fill labour vacancies. For example, an immigration law introduced in Germany in 2005 aimed to encourage highly skilled foreign workers to settle in the country. The host countries benefit because they have not had to bear the costs of educating and training their new workers.

Outside Europe, other MDCs depend on immigrant labour. Australia has the highest foreign-born population of any MDC – almost one in four of its people. Yet a report by a leading business information company in 2006 stated that the country needed to increase its intake of immigrants further to maintain economic growth.

◀ Some people move to Spain from northern European countries, such as these immigrants near the Costa Blanca. They usually immigrate because of the warm weather and comfortable lifestyle rather than because of work opportunities. These immigrants are taking an aerobics class near the Costa Blanca.

▲ MDCs are trying to encourage highly skilled workers, such as IT experts, to enter their countries.

summary

▶ Immigrants take resources away from local people and add to pressure on the environment. Immigrants are prepared to work for lower wages than local people, which means that the latter, particularly the poorly educated, lose their jobs to immigrants.

▶ Immigrants are good for the host economy and do not take jobs away from local workers. In fact, they often create businesses and increase job opportunities. They help to boost the working population, which is useful in countries where the population is declining.

CHAPTER 5

The effects of emigration

It is argued that emigration deprives LDCs of their best educated and highly skilled workers. This is called the 'brain drain'. Many countries have lost large proportions of their qualified citizens; for example, a quarter of Ghanaian and Iranian graduates have emigrated from their native countries.

The impact of the brain drain

The migration of more than 20,000 health professionals a year from sub-Saharan African countries is a serious problem. These nations are suffering from increasing poverty and the effects of HIV/AIDS, and require increased numbers of health workers. Yet they are losing many of these to HIV/AIDS and to emigration. While the LDCs have paid to educate and train these workers, the MDCs are benefiting from their skills. The departure of qualified people has an effect on the long-term development of the poorest countries. Some people argue that it is not ethical for MDCs to recruit them.

The brain drain from small Caribbean countries is the highest in the world. Here it has a significant effect because the populations are so much smaller than those of large sending countries such as India and China. In 2004, 75 per cent of Jamaicans with a degree lived outside the country (60 per cent of them had migrated to the USA). As a result, there is a large shortage of nurses and teachers in Jamaica.

Disruption of society

On an individual level, emigration disrupts family life for those remaining at home.

◀ There is an acute shortage of nurses in western countries. Hospitals such as this one in Paris, France, rely on immigrant nurses to staff their wards.

▲ This Chinese family lives in Australia. China is one of the main sources of emigrants worldwide, and there are Chinese people living in almost every country. Most Chinese migrants today are highly skilled professionals.

Women are often left to support their families, but many also migrate, leaving children to be cared for by grandparents, older siblings or friends. It is extremely hard for families to be separated in this way. Some experts argue that although people should have the right to emigrate, qualified workers should be able to lead a successful life in their own country.

The money sent home by migrants is clearly a major source of income for families. According to a 2003 World Bank report, in some rural areas of Jamaica 40 per cent of households receive income from family members working abroad. While this can help individual families and communities and sometimes may fund small business ventures, it does not necessarily spur economic growth and development at a national level. Also, it tends to encourage people to emigrate in search of a higher income when it could be more beneficial for them to stay and invest in their home country.

viewpoints

'The positive effects of remittances [money sent home] at the household level are clear, although not always undisputed. Unlike government to government aid, most remittances go directly to the family budget and are often used for basic subsistence needs [e.g. food] and better housing.'
Birnal Ghosh, International Organization for Migration, 2006

' . . . sometimes the best and the brightest leave. That has implications on the delivery of critical services, especially in the health sector; it has implications also for the intellectual capital [educated people] that the country needs for its own development.'
Dilip Ratha, a World Bank senior economist and expert on the brain drain, 2006

Remittances

People who emigrate from LDCs generally send a large part of their earnings home to their families – these money flows are called remittances. In 2004, US$144 billion (75 per cent of remittances worldwide) went to LDCs. And this is just the amount sent through official banking channels. Studies show that perhaps the same amount again is sent through informal channels, for example, with friends. Migrant workers from LDCs earn far more money in MDCs than they can at home, even in relatively low-paid jobs. For instance, professional Filipinos can earn more as cleaners in Europe than in their chosen careers in the Philippines.

Remittances can enrich whole communities. In African countries, receiving families will at first spend more on basics, such as food and household goods.

As the money continues to flow in, they spend it on health and improving their children's education. They may also invest in land or housing to provide some security for the family's future. People may pool their remittance money and use it to improve their community. In Mexico in the 1990s, farming communities invested in agricultural equipment that helped them to increase production.

It could be argued that the sending of remittances is bad for the host country. It would be better for the economy if the immigrants spent all their money there. However, the immigrants buy goods and services in the country they are living in, which helps the host economy.

▼ In Nattiobannigaripalle in India, a project in the early 2000s provided piped water and installed irrigation channels to water the rice fields. This project was supported by remittances.

case study

A better future?

Pozorrubio is a farming town in the Philippines. The people used to make a living there from growing sugarcane, rice and coconuts. But now they depend on remittances sent home by family members living and working abroad. As the former mayor, Noli Venezuela, comments: 'Now we grow big houses. This one's owned by a maid in Hong Kong. Across the street, she's a nanny in Canada.' There is a new park, paid for by maids, nannies and nurses working in Hong Kong. Filipino workers in Los Angeles, USA, have bought supplies for the hospital in Pozorrubio. The town has many new shops and businesses financed by remittances. Paying for education is a high priority too. Ms Salazar worked as a maid abroad and was able to use her earnings to send all of her five children to college. She says, 'Education is the reason we make this sacrifice. It hurt me to leave my children, but I did it to give them a better future.'

Largest recipients of remittances, 1990-2003

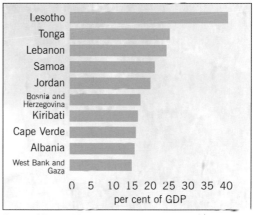

Countries where remittances form the largest proportion of GDP, 1990-2003

Source: *Migrants' Remittances and Development* by Bimal Ghosh, International Organization for Migration, 2006

Exporting talent

Some countries, such as India, produce more graduates than the economy requires, so emigration makes sense. India is a large country with a population of 1 billion, so the loss of a small proportion of its graduates does not necessarily have a negative effect on its economy. According to British migration expert Peter Stalker, around 25,000 graduates of the seven Indian Institutes of Technology, all prestigious institutions, are working in the USA. The export of talent may not represent a permanent loss. Some immigrants eventually return home with their skills and wealth.

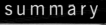

summary

▶ The brain drain means that LDCs lose highly skilled workers, which hinders their national economic development. It also causes disruption to family life.

▶ Emigration helps LDCs because emigrants send remittances that help improve the living standards of their families and local communities. It also provides opportunities for skilled people abroad who cannot find a job in their own country.

CHAPTER 6

Controlling immigration

Many people are concerned about 'opening the floodgates' and allowing in too many immigrants. Hortensia Barderas, a Spanish librarian living in Madrid, holds typical opinions and expresses the dilemma between what is fair and what is practical. She says Spain should not keep people out on the basis of where they are from. However, she says: 'if we let everyone in, if we open the doors completely, then we'll be overrun.' This viewpoint suggests that governments might want to limit the numbers allowed in and stop undocumented migrants entering the country.

EU countries may need to work together to control immigration. Some people argue that if one country fails to implement tough measures against undocumented migrants, then large numbers of immigrants will go there. If undocumented migrants succeed in entering Europe and are not deported (sent back), they will be able to travel freely throughout the EU. For example, the Spanish government estimated that 7,000 undocumented African migrants entered Spain between January and June 2006. In July 2006 the EU agreed to help Spain and other southern European countries stem the flow of migrants to their shores.

▼ Border patrol officers arrest undocumented Mexican migrants in Texas, along the border between the USA and Mexico.

▲ Newly arrived immigrants to Sweden are held in a reception centre while officials decide if they can stay in the country.

There are similar arguments in the USA. According to the Pew Hispanic Center's estimate, up to one million undocumented migrants enter the USA every year. Some people say the USA needs to tighten security along its border with Mexico, where most immigrants enter.

Highly skilled workers

People who argue for strict immigration controls believe that governments should only recruit those workers who are particularly needed for the country's economy. For example, in Australia and Canada there are skilled worker programmes to allow the controlled entry of highly qualified immigrants. In Germany there is a ban on the recruitment of unskilled and even moderately skilled workers. Highly skilled workers, however, can obtain a permanent settlement permit upon entering Germany.

It's a fact

In order to become an Australian citizen, a person must be a permanent resident of Australia and to have lived in the country for at least two of the previous five years. He or she must intend to reside there, be of good character, have a basic knowledge of English and understand the privileges and responsibilities of citizenship.

Alongside these strict immigration controls, rights to services such as health and education have been restricted in some countries so that not all immigrants can access them. In addition, governments in the UK, Germany and the Netherlands have introduced 'citizenship tests' to try to ensure that immigrants share the values of the host population. An opinion poll in Germany in 2006 showed that 79 per cent of Germans agreed that such tests were a good idea.

▲ Hispanic migrant workers in Sonoma County, California, picking and cutting grapes for wine production.

for the continuing poverty in many LDCs. Also, they say that the former colonial powers still have some responsibility towards the citizens of their ex-colonies.

Pro-immigration campaigners claim that fears of 'floods' of immigrants are exaggerated. The decision to migrate is very difficult and there would not be a huge wave of immigrants if controls were loosened or abandoned. Campaigners say there are strong humanitarian reasons for accepting migrants – it is important to protect people fleeing from conflict and persecution. MDCs have all signed international treaties committing them to defend human rights and offer protection to refugees and asylum seekers. Many people therefore see immigration controls as unfair and even racist. For example, in the Netherlands, only immigrants from outside the EU, North America and Australia have to pass the citizenship test.

Open the borders

There are some who argue that there is no need to tighten immigration controls. A few even argue that they are completely unnecessary. They hold that there are ethical as well as economic reasons why immigration rules should be relaxed to make it easier for people to move legally from country to country. They argue that MDCs have an important role in the world economy and are in some ways responsible

Unfair on the unskilled

Restrictive laws mean that it is extremely difficult for unskilled people to move legally to MDCs, so they are forced to seek an illegal route. Many argue that this is unjust. People only try to move to places where there is work, and where there are always jobs for unskilled workers when they arrive. Immigrants come to make a living, and if there are no jobs there will be no mass arrivals. Undocumented migrants often have to pay a people smuggler a vast sum of money to arrange a dangerous and uncertain journey to reach an MDC. And, even if they manage to reach their destination safely, they have to remain hidden from the authorities.

Undocumented migrants cannot complain to the authorities about their working conditions because they are not legally resident in a country. This means that they are frequently exploited by employers. For instance, a researcher in New York found a Chinese seamstress working more than 100 hours a week for less than US$2 (£1.10) an hour. There are reports of immigrants working without breaks for six or seven days a week, with no healthcare if they fall ill. Their human rights are not respected.

▼ Thousands of Nigerian women like Joy, who migrated to the city of Barcelona in Spain, were tricked into prostitution on their arrival.

Even worse, many thousands of undocumented migrants have been trafficked to MDCs. This means they have been tricked by people smugglers in their own country, who promise them good jobs if they migrate. On arrival in the new country the migrants are forced into criminal activities, such as prostitution, and must give most of their earnings to the smuggler. As they are undocumented migrants and must hide from the authorities, they find it hard to seek help.

Sometimes countries grant amnesty to undocumented migrants, giving them legal status. In 2005, Spain granted amnesty to 570,000 illegal migrants, the sixth amnesty in 20 years. Some people argue that it is sensible and ethical to allow all immigrants to live legally in their host country. Then they can have access to education and healthcare, learn the new language properly and play a more active role in society as well as being happier citizens.

summary

▶ Many people believe that strict immigration controls are necessary to limit the numbers of immigrants and to allow in only highly skilled workers. Without such controls, the MDCs could be overrun with immigrants.

▶ Others argue that workers will move wherever there are jobs and it is better to allow freedom of movement. There are important humanitarian reasons for allowing people to immigrate to escape persecution and live a better life.

CHAPTER 7

Does immigration cause racism?

One viewpoint states that if a country allows in a large number of immigrants it can lead to a rise in racial tension. Local people may feel threatened because the immigrants bring with them different cultural values. They may resent the immigrants because they believe they are competing for resources and jobs. Various groups have been the focus of resentment at different times, for example, Chinese immigrants to Australia in the late twentieth century.

Cultural differences

Much of the debate about immigration and race today focuses on cultural differences between the immigrants and the host population. For example, in many western nations, people are wary

It's a fact

The number of Muslims in France exceeds six million and represents 10 per cent of the population. They come from 53 countries and speak 21 languages. Algerians represent a great majority of Muslims in France. Some estimates show that the number of French Muslims will increase by more than threefold between 2006 and 2020. It is thought that their numbers will reach 20 million owing to the high fertility rate and birth rate, continuous immigration into France and the adoption of Islam by large numbers of French people. As of 2006, Muslims of purely French origin amounted to 100,000.

▼ In 2004, French Muslim women and their supporters demonstrated against the planned law to ban the wearing of the *hijab* (traditional head covering) in French schools. Despite opposition, the law was introduced.

▲ Jean-Marie Le Pen, leader of the extreme right-wing Front National party in France, addressing his supporters. His party opposes immigration.

weblinks

For more information about extremist political groups and immigration, go to www.waylinks.co.uk/Ethical Debates/immigration

of accepting more Muslims because they say they do not easily assimilate (fit in) with the existing society. The immigrants develop their own separate schools, shops, places of worship and community activities. Muslim women who follow Islamic custom wear a *hijab*, a headscarf, which clearly marks them out as different from the majority. France is a secular (non-religious) country by law. In 2004, the French government reinforced the secular principle by introducing a law that prohibited students from wearing the Muslim *hijab*, the Jewish *yarmulka* (skull cap) and large Christian crosses in schools. This led to a clash between the authorities and Muslims in particular, and caused rising racial tension between Muslims and non-Muslims.

Racism and the far right

Some people assert that the expansion of immigrant communities encourages the growth of extreme right-wing political parties. Then, they argue, far-right politicians link immigration to race in order to whip up fear and gain support. Such politicians blame the problems in society on non-white immigrants and people of immigrant origin who are citizens of the country. For instance, in 1995 in France, Jean-Marie Le Pen, the leader of the far-right Front National party, famously claimed that sending back three million immigrants would provide jobs for three million French people. Some people believe that the introduction of immigration restrictions could halt the growth of support for far-right parties that play on people's fear of foreigners. Therefore, they argue, tight immigration controls are morally justified,

Historical causes for racism

Some people do not agree that immigration causes racism. They believe it has historical causes. Between 1500 and 1900, Europeans enslaved Africans to work for them in the Americas (see page 10). Many Europeans developed the theory that white people were more intelligent than black people, and were born to rule. As European powers conquered countries around the world and ruled them as colonies, this viewpoint spread. Although the colonies gained independence in the twentieth century, for a minority of people the idea of white superiority has lived on.

Racism can also arise from current issues. Since the attacks on the World Trade Center in New York in September 2001, the USA has led a 'war on terror' to try to root out Islamic extremists in the world. The recent terrorist attacks have fuelled a general suspicion of Muslims in western countries. Making a negative judgement about people simply because they are Muslim is a form of racism, known as Islamophobia.

case study

Intolerant outburst

'A racist who branded a Muslim shopkeeper a terrorist on the day of the London bombings has been jailed. James McKeown, 37, of no fixed address, launched a tirade of abuse after spotting Mohammed Mahmood, who was wearing traditional Muslim dress, as he walked along Victoria Road, Cambridge, on July 7. McKeown shouted: "Look what you've done to London you terrorist, go back to your own country", before following him along the road hurling further abuse and threatening him with violence. Police said the incident was an unprovoked attack on a "very calm, quiet man", and welcomed McKeown's prison sentence. The 37-year-old was convicted of racially aggravated harassment at Cambridge Crown Court and jailed for 130 days.'

(*Cambridge Evening News*, 16 December 2005)

▼ French police arrest suspected rioters in Paris in 2005. The rioters were made up mostly of young black and Arab people of immigrant background who were angry and frustrated about their employment prospects.

▲ British Muslims at prayer in the backyard of a mosque in Oldham, northern England. Are separate faiths and cultures dividing society, or are they blamed unfairly for society's ills?

Sometimes, people blame immigrants for social problems, although the real reasons for these may be entirely different. When this happens, people may turn against immigrants, and there is a rise in racism. In 2005, riots broke out in France among black and Arab immigrant communities. The rioters were angry about the lack of jobs and opportunities they faced owing to racial discrimination. Government minister Nicolas Sarkozy (himself the son of a Hungarian immigrant) claimed the riots were caused by mass immigration. He introduced proposals to make it much harder for unskilled immigrants to settle in France and said that people who did not like the country could leave. In this atmosphere, public opinion polls showed growing support for the Front National.

viewpoints

'If we want to stop a very nasty surge of the extreme right, we have to deal seriously with this problem [immigration]'.
French member of parliament Jean Dionis du Séjour arguing in January 2006 that immigration should be restricted to qualified workers and promising students

'Today, the threat posed by 125 million displaced people, living either temporarily or permanently outside their countries of origin has replaced that which was posed by communism.'
Liz Fekete, deputy director of the Institute of Race Relations, speaking in 2001; Fekete says that immigrants and refugees are seen as the new world threat since the fall of the communist governments in 1989, and this is one reason why they suffer from racism

summary

▶ Some people say that a high level of immigration leads to increased racism.

▶ Other people believe there are wider historical and political causes for racism.

CHAPTER 8

Does immigration benefit society?

One argument states that a large number of immigrants can have a negative effect on society. Newcomers may have different customs and religions that conflict with local habits and alter the character of an area. Immigrants may find it hard to integrate at school and work, especially if they do not speak the language of the host country. For instance, Chinese immigrants in the USA and Australia, especially older people, struggle to learn English. According to a 2006 survey by Radio Netherlands: 'some 58 per cent of Europeans regard ethnic minorities as a threat'. Italy, Belgium and the Czech Republic score above the European average in their dislike of ethnic minorities.

High levels of immigration can divide the population. For example, US cities are segregated – different groups of people live in separate areas. Hispanics are spread throughout the USA, but they live overwhelmingly in neighbourhoods where they are the largest minority group. This kind of segregation can lead to tensions between different communities.

▼ In many major cities around the world there are Chinatowns - areas in which Chinese restaurants and shops can be found.This photo is of Chinatown in Philadelphia, USA.

▲ This is a Hispanic neighbourhood in Los Angeles, California, where the majority of inhabitants are from Latin American countries.

Crime and social problems

Anti-immigration campaigners in the USA claim that immigration has resulted in a wave of violent crime. For instance, in June 2003 it was reported that Adrian George Camacho shot dead a police officer who stopped his car. Camacho was a Mexican who had been in prison for attempted murder and drug offences. Some people commented that if the borders had been more tightly controlled, criminals like Camacho would not have been able to get into the country.

Such campaigners argue that social problems result from immigration. In Sweden, for example, unemployment levels are higher among the foreign-born than among natives of the country. Young immigrant people are more likely to drop out of school. Adult immigrants tend to be more dependent on social welfare (such as unemployment benefit) than are members of the host population, and are less likely

It's a fact

Population data from 41 US states indicates that the average non-Hispanic white person lives in a neighbourhood that is 6.3 per cent Hispanic. But the average Hispanic person lives in a neighbourhood that is 44 per cent Hispanic.

This kind of segregation can last for generations. Sociologist John Logan, who analysed the data, noted that the segregation of Jews and Italians in the USA declined after about 50 or 80 years. It could take until 2050 before Hispanics begin to be more integrated into US society.

than native people to vote in local elections. Their communities also experience a higher crime rate.

Those who oppose immigration insist that while people may want to emigrate to escape suffering in their own countries, governments must put the rights of their existing citizens first.

▲ Hasidic Jews stick closely to ancient Jewish religious traditions and live in their own communities. Most people in Europe and the USA are accepting of Hasidic Jews and their rights to follow their own traditions.

In contrast to the view that immigrants are responsible for crime, some people reason that immigrants are just the same as other groups in society. Such people argue that while a few immigrants may commit crime, the vast majority are law-abiding people. More immigrants are arrested, but this may be a result of discrimination by the police not the fact that they commit more crimes. And, while a tiny minority of immigrants may sympathize with terrorism, the perceived recent growth of terrorism may be the result of an extreme response to the wars led by the USA and the UK against Muslim countries such as Afghanistan and Iraq.

People also argue that there are good reasons why immigrants tend to use more welfare services. In Sweden, immigrants experience higher rates of unemployment because most of them are refugees. In 1972, the Swedish government halted the immigration of workers from non-Nordic countries, while still allowing refugees to come. Many of the refugees are from the former Yugoslavia, Iran and Iraq. It takes time for these people to be integrated into society. They are generally poorer, which is why they rely more on social welfare. In time, it is argued, they will be able to make their contribution to society.

weblinks

For information about famous immigrants to the USA, go to www.waylinks.co.uk/Ethical Debates/immigration

Segregation or integration?

Time is important in the case of segregation too. In the past, similar complaints about immigrants and alien cultures were expressed against the Jews in the USA. For example, between 1881 and 1914, about two million Jews migrated from Russia and eastern Europe to the USA. Many Americans were concerned about high numbers of Jews in New York and about their different style of dress, customs and religious worship. Yet over time these immigrant people became integrated into society and made significant contributions in the fields of law, medicine, science, education, literature, music, film, theatre and art. Pro-immigration campaigners argue that the same will happen with newer groups of immigrants. They say that a humane society should support the right of people to make a better life elsewhere. Many people from MDCs migrate to other countries. It is therefore important that others, if they want to, should be allowed to migrate to MDCs.

▲ World-famous orchestral conductor Zubin Mehta shown here with the Vienna Philharmonic Orchestra. Mehta moved from Mumbai, India, to the USA when he was 18 years of age.

It's a fact

Famous immigrants to the USA include Elie Wiesel (Romania), scholar of Jewish studies and Nobel Prize winner; the great basketball player Hakeem Olajuwon (Nigeria); the orchestra conductor Zubin Mehta (India); the former US Secretary of State Madeleine Albright (Czech Republic); the author Isabel Allende (Chile); the film director Wayne Wang (China); and Jeong H. Kim (South Korea), who created a highly successful technology company.

Loss of national identity

There is a common view that it is important to have a shared culture and loyalty within a country. British journalist Peter Hitchens maintains that immigration to the UK was extremely limited in the past. Now he says, there is a huge level of uncontrolled illegal immigration 'conservatively estimated at 100,000 a year' (2003). He argues that rather than becoming multicultural, Britain now has no culture and all of its traditions are being forgotten. People are concerned that their national identity is on the verge of being lost and 'swamped' by foreign influences.

Similar fears are expressed by a large number of Dutch people, particularly with regard to Islam. According to a 2004 survey by Radio Netherlands, out of 1,020 native Dutch people, 50 per cent said they were concerned about immigration and its influence on Dutch society. In the Dutch town of Alphen Aan Den Rijn, employment office worker Ibolya Fransen believes that Muslims, with their own shops and places of worship, are threatening her way of life: 'In my town, we have a population of 70,000, but we already have two mosques. In five years' time it will be three or four. They will take over.'

▲ In 2006, the Essalam Mosque was under construction in Rotterdam in the Netherlands. Once completed, it will be the biggest mosque in Western Europe, holding 1,500 worshippers.

▲ This Roma family are at a Roma campsite north of Paris. They live in terrible conditions and are constantly forced to move on. They hope to move to the UK in the belief that life will be easier there.

In western countries, there have been heightened concerns about terrorism in recent years, following the attacks on the USA of 11 September 2001. Some people believe that immigrants, or indeed people of immigrant origin, may not be loyal to their host country. The fear is that some of these people may support terrorism. In July 2005, a series of suicide bombings were carried out in London by Muslim men born and brought up in the UK. In June 2006, seven Muslim US citizens were arrested, accused of planning to blow up the Sears Tower in Chicago, Illinois.

A richer society

Countries do not share a single culture but contain a mixture of cultures because of waves of immigration that have taken place over the centuries. Over time, a cultural exchange takes place between local people and immigrants, with each influencing the other. For example, hip-hop music developed in the USA from the Jamaican practice of 'toasting' (talking or chanting over the rhythms of popular songs). Since the 1980s, hip-hop has spread all over the world, including to Latin America, Asia and Africa. In Europe, both local people and immigrants produce hip-hop music.

Food is another obvious example. In the multicultural cities of MDCs people can eat food from all around the world. In Chicago, USA, it is possible to choose from American hamburger restaurants, Jewish bagel bakeries, Cajun fried chicken cafés, Spanish tapas bars, Japanese sushi bars (see below), Mexican taco bars and dozens more styles of food outlets.

▼ Many of the most popular restaurants in western countries, such as this sushi restaurant in the USA, are run by immigrants.

Education

Many believe that it is advantageous for children to grow up among people from different cultures. Priya, a 16-year-old British Asian, says: 'I think mixing people from different backgrounds is a wonderful and crucial thing to do. Wherever somebody lives there will always be different types of people, so mixing them, especially in schools, is vital. By learning about different cultures you have a better understanding of yourself.'

Those in favour of immigration say this shows that immigrants make a country richer economically and culturally. They say it is important to look at the benefits and remember that there has always been international migration, but immigration controls are a twentieth-century development.

▲ Immigrants have brought their music and dance to their new countries. Here, an English couple take a Latin American salsa dance class.

summary

▶ Some people argue that immigrants cause social problems; these people say that limits should be imposed on immigration.

▶ Other people argue that immigrants are a positive benefit to society and should therefore be welcomed.

case study

Faïza Guène

Young French author Faïza Guène was born to Algerian immigrants in France. She grew up on the public housing estates in Pantin, outside Paris. At the age of 13, Faïza started to attend the neighbourhood cultural centre and began to write a novel about a teenage girl growing up with her Moroccan mother in a poor suburb of Paris. Called *Just Like Tomorrow*, the book expressed the hardships of immigrant life but also the positive aspects of life in the suburbs. One of the founders of the centre read the first 40 pages of the novel and showed it to his sister, who worked for a publishing company. She was so impressed that she put it forward for publication. The book proved extraordinarily successful; 200,000 copies were sold in France and it became a set text in schools in 2006.

Glossary

Alien Foreign, or from a foreign country.

Amnesty An official pardon for an offence.

Asylum seeker A person who has fled his or her country and is claiming asylum (protection as a refugee in a safe country).

Citizenship Membership of a state, either as a person born there or as an immigrant who has gained membership; citizenship involves certain rights and responsibilities.

Discrimination Treating people unfairly, for example, because of their skin colour, religion, gender or age.

Emigrate To leave one's own country to settle permanently in another.

Ethnic group A group set apart from others because of its national or racial origin or culture.

Ethnic minority A group set apart from the majority in society because of its national or racial origin or culture.

Front National A right-wing political party in France that opposes immigration.

GDP Gross Domestic Product – the total value of goods and services produced within the borders of a country.

Hispanic A Spanish-speaking person from Latin America or from a Latin American family, living in the USA.

HIV/AIDS A disease of the human immune system resulting from infection by a virus.

Host population The local people in a country to which immigrants come.

Legal immigrant An immigrant who has permission to settle in another country or an undocumented migrant who has won the legal right to settle.

Less Developed Countries (LDCs) The poorer countries of the world, including the countries of Africa, Asia (except for Japan), Latin America and the Caribbean.

Migrant worker A person who moves to another country for a limited period to work.

More Developed Countries (MDCs) The richer countries of the world, including Europe and northern America.

Multicultural Involving several ethnic groups and cultures.

Net migration The difference between immigration into and emigration from an area; for example, if 300,000 people enter a country and 200,000 leave, there is net migration of 100,000 into the country.

Nordic Refers to the north-western European countries of Scandinavia, Iceland and Finland.

Persecution The cruel treatment of people, for example, because of their race, religion or political beliefs.

Quota The number of immigrants allowed to enter a country each year.

Refugee A person who seeks safety from war, natural disaster or ill-treatment in another country.

Right-wing The side of a political system that is more traditional, including people who generally do not welcome change.

Roma A travelling people who originally came from India but now live mostly in Europe.

Segregation Describes a situation in which different ethnic groups live in separate areas.

Service industries Industries, such as hotels, catering and transport, that provide services rather than making goods.

Sociologist Someone who studies human societies and the way in which they function.

Undocumented migrant Someone who has not entered the country according to the immigration laws.

United Nations (UN) An organization founded at the end of the Second World War, with the aim of preventing future wars.

World Bank An international banking organization that makes loans to countries when they have economic problems.

Timeline

3rd century BC Emperor of China builds a wall to keep out neighbouring tribes.

AD 1442 Portuguese start to enslave Africans.

1492 Spanish monarchs expel Jews and Muslims from Spain.

c.1550 Europeans start to transport enslaved Africans to the Americas to work.

1596 Queen Elizabeth I orders that all Africans be expelled from England.

1788 British government begins to send convicts to Australia.

From c.1830 Indentured workers (who have borrowed money), mostly from China, India and the Pacific region, emigrate to European colonies.

From c.1850 Voluntary mass emigration to the Americas begins.

1882 Chinese Exclusion Act passed in the USA.

1901 Immigration Restriction Act in Australia ends non-European immigration; it becomes known as the White Australia Policy.

1905 Aliens Act passed in Britain.

1924 Immigration Act in the USA permits the immigration of a quota of people from each sending country.

post-1945 Mass emigration of Europeans to Australia.

1950s and 1960s France and UK invite immigrants from their former colonies.

1961 Germany invites 'guest workers' into the country.

1962 Immigration Act in UK introduces restrictions on immigrants.

1965 Immigration and Nationality Act in the USA abolishes the system of national quotas.

1967 Canada introduces a points system for potential immigrants.

1972 Sweden introduces a law to prevent immigrants from non-Nordic countries from entering.

1973 Economic crisis in Europe leads to restrictions on immigration.

1973 End of the White Australia Policy; all immigrants are permitted to apply for citizenship after living in Australia for three years.

1986 US law imposes penalties on employers who hire undocumented migrants and offers an amnesty to three million undocumented migrants already in the country.

1999 Large numbers of Ecuadorians move to Spain because of economic crisis in Ecuador.

February 2004 French government bans school children from wearing obvious religious symbols, such as the Muslim headscarf.

May 2004 European Union is expanded from 15 to 25 members; the UK, Ireland and Sweden permit immigration from the new member countries.

January 2005 Germany introduces a new immigration law that restricts unskilled or semi-skilled workers but encourages highly skilled immigrants.

November 2005 British citizenship test for immigrants comes into force.

December 2005 Immigration law HR 4437 is passed in the USA.

2006 Finland, Spain and Portugal lift restrictions on Eastern European immigrants from the European Union.

February 2006 The German state of Baden-Württemberg introduces a citizenship test.

March 2006 Language and cultural awareness tests are introduced in the Netherlands.

May 2006 Protests in the USA against immigration law HR 4437.

Further information

Books to read include:

Immigrants and Refugees
Cath Senker
(Orchard Books, 2004)

World Issues: Immigration
Ruth Wilson
(Franklin Watts, 2004)

Useful organizations include:

Australian Refugee Council
PO Box 946, Glebe, NSW 2037, Australia

Joint Council for the Welfare of Immigrants
115 Old Street, London EC1V 9RT, UK

National Immigration Forum
50 F Street NW, Suite 300, Washington,
DC 20001, USA

Index

ETHICAL DEBATES

Contents of titles in the series: